Cooking Herbs

Add Fresh Flavor to your Food and Discover 40 Superb Herb Recipes

BY

Daniel Humphreys

License Notes

No part of this Book can be reproduced in any form or by any means including print, electronic, scanning or photocopying unless prior permission is granted by the author.

All ideas, suggestions and guidelines mentioned here are written for informative purposes. While the author has taken every possible step to ensure accuracy, all readers are advised to follow information at their own risk. The author cannot be held responsible for personal and/or commercial damages in case of misinterpreting and misunderstanding any part of this Book

Table of Contents

Introduction...7

Appetizers and Lite Bites....................................10

    Citrus and Cilantro Shrimp............................... 11

    Clams in Buttery Herb Sauce........................... 13

    Garden Herb Omelet.. 15

    Grilled Halloumi with Fresh Herbs and Strawberries... 17

    Honey Mustard Egg Salad Toast 20

    Pistachio, Cranberry, and Mint Goat Cheese Log 22

    Ricotta Crostini with Sorrel Pesto.............................. 24

    Summer Salad with Oregano and Orange Dressing 26

    Tortilla Ball Soup.. 29

    White Wine Asparagus Risotto with Chervil............... 32

Mains... 35

    Basil and Mushroom Gnocchi 36

    Beef Tenderloin Roast with Horseradish Sauce 39

    Beef Meatballs in Creamy Herb Sauce 43

    Duck Roasted in Lavender Honey 47

    Halibut with Herb Sauce 51

    Lemon Tofu with Thyme 54

    Pork Chops in Garlic and Herb Wine Sauce 57

    Roma-Style Lamb with Rosemary, Sage, and Anchovy 61

    Sweet Potato and Fennel Curry 65

    Vietnamese Lemongrass Chicken 68

Sauces and Sides 71

    Cucumber and Mint Jelly 72

    Garlic Herb Sauce 76

    Grilled Corn with a Mixed Herb Dressing 79

Hasselback Sweet Potatoes with Compound Mixed Herb Ghee 83

Lemon Balm Pesto 86

Pan-Fried Carrots with Lemon and Marjoram 88

Roasted Beets with Pistachios, Mixed Herbs, and Orange 91

Roasted Cauliflower with Herbs and Spices 95

Summer Savory Green Beans with Mushrooms and Bacon 98

Take-Out Kebab Garlic Sauce 101

Desserts 103

Bay Leaf Rice Pudding with Golden Raisins 104

Bitter Chocolate Basil Tart 107

Citrus Sorrel Sherbet 110

Lavender and Walnut Blondies 113

Nectarine Thyme Crumble 116

Pineapple Mint Granita 119

Rosemary Melon Sorbet 121

Sage and Cranberry Cookies 123

Tarragon Berry Tumble with Anise Oat Topping 126

Vanilla and Garlic Ice Cream 129

Author's Afterthoughts 132

About the Author 133

Introduction

Incorporating herbs into everyday cooking is becoming increasingly popular.

You can buy lots of different types of herbs, both dried and fresh. Buy them from your store, farm fresh at your local farmer's market, or even grow them in your own garden.

Fresh herbs have great flavor and fragrance and although they have a shorter shelf-life than dried, they are well worth including in your family meals. Whereas dried herbs are an invaluable food cupboard staple and can be an inexpensive and convenient way to pep up every day dishes; both sweet and savory.

Different types of herbs bring a different flavor to the table and pair exceptionally well with certain recipes.

For instance, fennel's distinct licorice flavor is perfect in a veggie curry, whereas chervil complements a rice risotto and lavender elevates a honey sauce to new levels.

What's more, cooking with herbs can provide your body with healthy antioxidants.

Many fresh herbs contain such a high level of antioxidants that, even when they are dried, they are still super healthy.

Super herbs include sage, thyme, marjoram, oregano and basil.

For instance, just ½ teaspoon of dried oregano has the same antioxidant content as ½ cup of sweet potato!

In fact, Cooking with Herbs is the best way to add flavor to food in a healthy and additive-free way.

Appetizers and Lite Bites

Citrus and Cilantro Shrimp

A vibrant and flavorsome dish bursting with zesty citrus flavor, perfect for your summer get-togethers.

Servings: 4-6

Total Time: 5mins

Ingredients:

- 2 tsp soy sauce
- 1 tbsp hot sauce
- 2 tsp olive oil
- Pinch sugar
- Zest and juice of 2 lemons, 2 oranges, 2 limes
- 12 ounces cooked shrimp (peeled)
- ¼ cup fresh cilantro (roughly chopped)

Directions:

1. Combine the soy sauce, hot sauce, olive oil, sugar, citrus zest, and juice in a bowl.

2. Add the shrimp and toss well.

3. Transfer to a serving platter and garnish with plenty of fresh cilantro.

Clams in Buttery Herb Sauce

Serve with plenty of fresh crusty bread to mop up the indulgent, rich buttery herb sauce.

Servings: 4

Total Time: 15mins

Ingredients:

- 4 tbsp butter
- 3 tbsp minced shallot
- 1 tsp crushed red pepper flakes
- 3 tbsp minced garlic
- 1 cup white wine
- 36 littleneck clams (cleaned and scrubbed)
- 2 tbsp fresh mint (chopped)
- 2 tbsp fresh tarragon (chopped)
- Crusty bread (sliced, to serve)

Directions:

1. Melt the butter in a pot over the moderate heat. Add the shallot, sauté for 2 minutes. Then add the red pepper and garlic, sauté until the garlic releases its aroma.

2. Pour in the wine and cook for 2 minutes before tossing in the clams. Cover with a lid and allow to steam for 5-6 minutes, until the clams open.

3. Throw away any closed clams. Stir in the mint and tarragon.

4. Serve with crusty bread.

Garden Herb Omelet

What's not to love about a fluffy, golden omelet flavored with aromatic garden herbs and Parmesan cheese?!

Servings: 1

Total Time: 10mins

Ingredients:

- 2 eggs
- 2 leaves basil (torn)
- 2 tsp fresh chives (snipped)
- Leaves of 1 thyme sprig (torn)
- Salt and black pepper
- 1 tbsp butter
- 1 tbsp Parmesan cheese (grated)

Directions:

1. Whisk the eggs until fluffy. Stir in the herbs and season well.

2. Melt the butter in a skillet over moderately high heat. Pour in the eggs and swirl the pan.

3. Using a rubber spatula, push the cooked eggs to the center while tilting the skillet.

4. When almost set, after approximately 6 minutes, sprinkle with the Parmesan.

5. Fold the cooked omelet in half and transfer to a plate. Enjoy.

Grilled Halloumi with Fresh Herbs and Strawberries

The saltiness of grilled halloumi is perfectly balanced with the sweetness of fresh marinated strawberries and refreshing mint and cilantro.

Servings: 4

Total Time: 20mins

Ingredients:

Strawberries:

- 2 tbsp lime juice
- 3 tbsp olive oil
- 1 serrano chile (seeded, minced)
- Black pepper
- 2 tsp agave nectar
- 6 ounces fresh strawberries (hulled, chopped)

Halloumi:

- 1 tbsp oil
- 8 ounces halloumi (sliced into 8 pieces)
- 2 tbsp fresh cilantro (chopped)
- 2 tbsp fresh mint (chopped)

Directions:

1. Whisk together the lime juice, olive oil, chile, black pepper, and agave nectar in a bowl. Add the chopped strawberries and toss to coat. Set to one side.

2. Heat the oil in a skillet over moderately high heat, add the slices of halloumi and cook for a few minutes without touching the cheese. The cheese should have a golden crust.

3. Arrange the cheese on a serving platter, top with the strawberry mixture and sprinkle with the fresh cilantro and mint. Enjoy straight away.

Honey Mustard Egg Salad Toast

A herby homemade egg salad served on toasted seed bread is a comforting and satisfying lunchtime treat.

Servings: 4

Total Time: 10mins

Ingredients:

- 4 tbsp sour cream
- 4 tbsp mayonnaise
- 1 tsp organic honey
- 2 tsp Dijon mustard
- 2 tbsp minced scallions
- 1 tbsp minced shallots
- 2 tbsp fresh lovage (chopped)
- Salt and black pepper
- 8 hard-boiled eggs (peeled, lightly mashed)
- 4 slices seeded bread (toasted)

Directions:

1. In a bowl, whisk together the sour cream, mayo, honey, and mustard until combined.

2. Stir in the scallions, shallots, and lovage, then season with salt and black pepper.

3. Carefully fold in the mashed egg until combined.

4. Spoon the egg salad onto toast and serve.

Pistachio, Cranberry, and Mint Goat Cheese Log

A delicious appetizer that looks almost as good as it tastes. What's more, it can be prepared in under 5 minutes, perfect for those last minute guests!

Servings: 6

Total Time: 5mins

Ingredients:

- 2 tbsp fresh mint (chopped)
- 2 tbsp toasted pistachios (chopped)
- 2 tbsp dried cranberries
- 1 log goat cheese
- Organic honey
- Crackers (to serve)

Directions:

1. Combine the mint, nuts, and cranberries on a plate.

2. Roll the goat cheese log in the mixture to evenly coat.

3. Arrange the cheese on a serving platter and drizzle with honey. Serve with crackers.

Ricotta Crostini with Sorrel Pesto

Forget basil, from now on you will only ever want your pesto made with sorrel! This yummy crostini dish is both simple and quick, perfect for those spontaneous get-togethers.

Servings: 10-12

Total Time: 10mins

Ingredients:

Sorrel Pesto:

- ¼ cup fresh parsley
- ¾ cup fresh sorrel
- 1 cup olive oil
- 1 clove garlic (peeled)
- Salt and black pepper

Crostini:

- 2 cups fresh ricotta cheese
- French baguette (sliced, toasted)

Directions:

1. Add the parsley, sorrel, oil, and garlic to a food processor. Blitz until smooth and season to taste.

2. Spoon an equal amount of ricotta cheese onto the slices of baguette and drizzle each portion with plenty of fresh pesto. Serve.

Summer Salad with Oregano and Orange Dressing

A fresh summer salad drizzled with a homemade orange and oregano dressing is the perfect accompaniment to your favorite dishes or can even be enjoyed on its own.

Servings: 3-4

Total Time: 30mins

Ingredients:

Dressing:

- ½ cup freshly squeezed orange juice
- 1 tsp red wine vinegar
- 1 tbsp olive oil
- 1 tbsp fresh oregano (chopped)
- ¾ tsp kosher salt

Salad:

- 1 head radicchio (torn)
- 2 tbsp fresh coriander leaves
- 3 oranges (peeled, membranes removed, sliced)
- ½ cup red onion (thinly sliced)

Directions:

1. First, make the dressing. Add the orange juice to a saucepan and cook for 5-6 minutes over high heat until it reduces to approximately 2 tbsp. Allow to cool.

2. Combine the concentrated juice with the vinegar, oil, oregano, and salt.

3. Prepare the salad. Toss together the radicchio, coriander leaves, oranges, and red onion in a serving bowl.

4. Drizzle over the dressing and toss again. Serve.

Tortilla Ball Soup

This delicious Mexican soup dish is brought to life with fresh and earthy epazote.

Servings: 6-8

Total Time: 50mins

Ingredients:

- 1 cup whole milk
- 1 pound stale corn tortillas (torn into pieces)
- 6 fresh epazote leaves (chopped)
- 2 ounces cotija cheese (grated)
- 1 onion (peeled, chopped)
- 1 clove garlic (peeled)
- Yolk of 1 egg
- 1 egg
- Salt and black pepper
- 3 ounces lard
- 6 tbsp tomato puree
- 8 cups beef stock
- ½ cup heavy cream

Directions:

1. Pour the milk into a bowl and add the tortillas. Allow to soak for half an hour.

2. Transfer the soaked tortillas to a food processor along with the epazote, cotija, onion, garlic, yolk, egg, salt, and black pepper. Blitz until smooth. Roll the mixture into 2" balls.

3. In a saucepan over moderately high heat, melt the lard. Add the balls to the lard and cook for 5 minutes, turning as need. Set the tortilla balls to one side.

4. To the same pan, add the tomato puree and cook for a couple of minutes. Pour in the beef stock along with a pinch of seasoning and bring to a boil, allow to simmer for 10 minutes.

5. Stir in the cream and return the tortilla balls to the soup. Allow to cook for 5 minutes before serving.

White Wine Asparagus Risotto with Chervil

Who doesn't love a thick and creamy risotto? This delicious offering with fresh green asparagus and herby chervil makes a fantastic appetizer or light dish.

Servings: 6-8

Total Time: 45mins

Ingredients:

- 4 cups chicken stock
- 2 tbsp olive oil
- ½ yellow onion (peeled, diced)
- 1½ cups Arborio rice
- ¼ cup white wine
- 14 ounces fresh asparagus (tips trimmed, peeled, stems sliced ¼" thick)
- ¼ cup country butter
- 3 tbsp Parmesan cheese (grated)
- 6 sprigs fresh chervil (chopped finely)

Directions:

1. Bring the chicken stock to a simmer in a saucepan and keep warm.

2. In a saucepan over high heat, add the oil. When hot, add the onion and sauté for 5-6 minutes.

3. Add the rice, stir well and cook for 60 seconds. Pour in the wine and cook for another 60 seconds.

4. Pour in enough chicken stock to just cover the rice and bring the mixture to the boil. Turn the heat down to moderately low and while continually stirring, replenish the stock as is it absorbed by the rice for approximately 25 minutes, until the rice is al dente. If you run out of stock, use hot water.

5. For the final 5 minutes of cooking, stir in the asparagus tips and sliced stems, followed by the butter, Parmesan, and chervil.

6. Serve.

Mains

Basil and Mushroom Gnocchi

Tender little Italian potato dumplings are cooked in butter, white wine, basil, and lemon juice and tossed with earthy mushrooms for a dish you'll be whipping up time and time again.

Servings: 2

Total Time: 30mins

Ingredients:

- 8 ounces fresh gnocchi
- 4 tbsp butter
- 4 ounces mushrooms (stems removed, chopped)
- Salt and black pepper
- 2 garlic cloves (peeled, minced)
- ½ cup white wine
- Juice of ½ a lemon
- ½ cup fresh basil (chopped)
- Shavings Parmesan cheese (for serving)

Directions:

1. Cook the gnocchi according to packet instructions and set to one side when cooked.

2. In the meantime, melt half of the butter in a pan over moderate heat. When it begins to bubble, add the mushrooms, season well. Sauté for 5 minutes.

3. Add the garlic and sauté for another 60 seconds.

4. Pour in the white wine to deglaze the pan. Cook until half of the wine has evaporated.

5. Add the cooked gnocchi to the pan along with the remaining butter, lemon juice, and basil.

6. Cook for a final couple of minutes, while swirling the pan.

7. Transfer to bowls and top with shavings of Parmesan.

Beef Tenderloin Roast with Horseradish Sauce

Enjoy the very best tender roast beef with a mixed herb rub served with a tasty horseradish sauce; perfect for any get-together with family or friends.

Servings: 4

Total Time: 11hours 20mins

Ingredients:

- 2 tsp dried oregano leaves
- 2 tsp dried thyme
- 2 tsp dried rosemary (crushed)
- 1 tsp dry mustard
- 2 tsp garlic powder
- 2 tsp coarse sea salt
- ½ tsp freshly ground black pepper
- 2½ pounds beef tenderloin roast (trimmed, tied)
- 1 tbsp olive oil

Horseradish Sauce:

- ½ cup sour cream
- 3 tbsp low-fat mayonnaise
- Horseradish (prepared, to taste)
- Pinch salt
- Dash of Worcestershire sauce
- Spring of fresh thyme (to garnish)

Directions:

1. 4-5 hours before you plan to cook the beef, prepare the rub.

2. In a bowl, combine the oregano with the thyme, rosemary, mustard, garlic powder, 2 teaspoons of sea salt and pepper.

3. Evenly coat the beef with the mixture and completely wrap using kitchen wrap. Transfer the beef to the fridge for 4 hours, to allow the spices to intensify.

4. An hour before you intend to roast the meat, remove the roast from the fridge, and set aside at room temperature.

5. Preheat the main oven to 450 degrees F.

6. Take the kitchen wrap off the meat and arrange the roast on a rack in a roasting pan. Rub the meat all over with olive oil.

7. Transfer the roast to the oven and sear; this will seal in the meat juices and take around 15 minutes. The roast should be brown on the outside.

8. Reduce the oven temperature to 325 degrees F and continue to roast until you achieve your preferred level of doneness. For medium rare, cook for 27 minutes, or until a meat thermometer put into the thickest part of the meat registers 135 degrees F.

9. When the meat is sufficiently cooked to your liking remove the roast from the oven, tent using aluminum foil and before carving, set aside for 12-15 minutes.

10. While the meat rests, make the sauce. In a bowl, combine the sour cream with the mayonnaise, horseradish, and season with a pinch of salt and a dash of Worcestershire sauce.

11. Serve the sauce with the carved meat, garnish with thyme and enjoy.

Beef Meatballs in Creamy Herb Sauce

Creamy white wine and chive sauce is perfect when served with juicy beef meatballs and fresh pasta.

Servings: 4

Total Time: 40mins

Ingredients:

- 1 pound ground beef
- 5 ounces cheese with garlic and herbs (crumbled)
- ¾ tsp salt
- ¼ tsp black pepper
- Oil
- 1 small yellow onion (peeled, thinly chopped)
- 2 tbsp all-purpose flour
- 3½ cups low salt chicken broth
- 8 ounces fresh egg noodles
- ¼ cup white wine
- ¼ cup fresh chives (finely chopped)

Directions:

1. In a bowl, combine the beef with the cheese, followed by ¾ tsp salt and ¼ tsp of black pepper, gently kneading until incorporated.

2. Mold the mixture into 1" meatballs.

3. Over moderate to high heat, in a large skillet heat the oil until smoking.

4. Add the meatballs and cook until brown all over, this will take around 5 minutes.

5. Transfer the meatballs to a plate and pour off the fat from the pan, setting aside 1 tbsp of fat.

6. Cook the onion in the 1 tbsp of fat, for 5-7 minutes, until browned.

7. Stir in the flour, cooking until golden for approximately 60 seconds.

8. Add the broth followed by the noodles and wine and bring to boil.

9. Cover with a lid and turn the heat down to moderately low,

10. Cook while frequently stirring until the pasta cooks, for 5 minutes.

11. Add the meatballs and bring to simmer, while covered, until the meatballs are sufficiently cooked through, and the noodles are al dente, approximately 4-5 minutes.

12. While the pan is removed from the heat, add the remaining cheese and chive and stir to combine.

13. Season and serve.

Duck Roasted in Lavender Honey

This super sophisticated dish will impress both family and friends at your next dinner party.

Servings: 4

Total Time: 2hours 30mins

Ingredients:

- ½ tsp black pepper
- 1 tbsp thyme leaves
- 1 tsp sea salt
- 4 tbsp culinary-grade dried lavender
- 1 (4½ pound) whole duck
- 3½ cups chicken broth
- ½ cup red wine vinegar
- 2 tbsp lavender honey
- Roasted vegetables (to serve)

Directions:

1. Preheat the main oven to 400 degrees F.

2. Grind together the black pepper, thyme, salt, and 2 tbsp lavender.

3. Score the breast part of the whole duck with a knife in a criss-cross pattern.

4. Rub the whole duck with half of the ground mixture. Transfer to a roasting tin and place in the oven. Cook for 1 hour and 45 minutes.

5. Take out of the oven and set the duck to one side.

6. Pour any extra fat out of the tin, then place it over moderate heat. Add the chicken broth and vinegar to the tin and bring to the boil.

7. Place the duck back in the tin, basting it with the broth mixture. Brush the duck with 1 tbsp of lavender honey.

8. Put back in the oven for another 15 minutes to caramelize. Remember to baste the duck a few times during the final cook. Brush it with the last tbsp of lavender honey and sprinkle with the remaining ground herb mixture.

9. Take the duck out of the oven, cut into 8 pieces and transfer to a serving platter. Pour over the juices from the roasting tin. Serve with roasted vegetables.

Halibut with Herb Sauce

A simple fish main course that is ready in under 20 minutes makes a perfect midweek meal.

Servings: 6

Total Time: 18mins

Ingredients:

- 6 tbsp freshly squeezed lemon juice
- 6 tbsp extra-virgin olive oil
- 3 tbsp chopped fresh chives
- 3 tbsp chopped fresh basil
- 3 tbsp chopped fresh parsley
- Salt and freshly ground black pepper
- 6 (6 ounce) halibut fillets
- 2 tbsp olive oil

Directions:

1. Add the lemon juice, olive oil, chives, basil and parsley to a food processor and puree. Season with salt and pepper.

2. Preheat your broiler.

3. Brush the halibut with 2 tbsp of oil and season with salt and pepper.

4. Broil the fish until the center is just opaque, approximately 5 minutes each side.

5. Transfer the halibut to dinner plates.

6. Spoon the herb sauce over the top and serve.

Lemon Tofu with Thyme

The chewy texture of the tofu is complemented by the combination of the acidic flavors of apple cider vinegar and freshly squeezed lemon juice. The soy sauce adds salt, while the thyme adds an earthy yet minty undertone.

Servings: 2

Total Time: 55mins

Ingredients:

- 1 pound extra-firm tofu
- 2 tbsp freshly squeezed lemon juice
- ½ tbsp apple cider vinegar
- 2 tbsp soy sauce
- 2 tbsp olive oil
- 2 tsp thyme (chopped)
- Black pepper

Directions:

1. Preheat the main oven to 475 degrees F.

2. Wrap the tofu in kitchen paper towels and gently press by adding weight on top of the tofu for 10 minutes.

3. Remove the kitchen towel from the tofu and slice the tofu into pieces of no more than ½" thick.

4. In a bowl, combine the lemon juice with the vinegar, soy sauce, olive oil, and thyme. Add a dash of black pepper.

5. Transfer the tofu, in a single layer, to a casserole dish. Cover the tofu with the lemon juice mixture, turning once to coat evenly.

6. Bake in the oven for between 30-40 minutes or until browned, turning only once halfway through baking. The secret to the success of this dish is to avoid opening the oven door too many times.

Pork Chops in Garlic and Herb Wine Sauce

Pork can be especially hard to spice-up, but by adding thyme to a white wine sauce, you will enhance the flavors of an already delicious meal.

Servings: 4

Total Time: 35mins

Ingredients:

- ¼ cup all-purpose flour
- ½ tsp garlic powder
- ½ tsp onion powder
- 1 tsp Italian seasoning
- Salt and freshly ground pepper
- 4 boneless pork chops
- 2 tbsp butter

Creamy Herb and Wine Sauce:

- 2 tbsp butter
- 2 cloves garlic (peeled, minced)
- 1 tbsp flour
- ½ cup dry white wine
- Freshly squeezed juice of ¼ lemon
- ½ cup chicken stock
- ½ cup heavy cream
- 1 tsp Italian seasoning
- 4 sprigs fresh thyme (leaves only)

Directions:

1. In a mixing bowl, whisk the flour along with the garlic and onion powder followed by the Italian seasoning. Liberally season with salt and freshly ground black pepper.

2. Dredge the chops in the flour mixture, coating on both sides.

3. In a large frying pan or skillet, melt the butter over moderately high heat.

4. When the pan is sufficiently hot, add the dredged pork chops, searing them. Cook on one side on moderate-high heat for 3-4 minutes, reduce the heat to moderate and cook on the reverse side for 1-2 minutes.

5. Take the pan off the heat and transfer the cooked pork to a serving plate. Cover the plate and keep the chops warm.

6. Next, prepare the sauce: Place the frying pan back on the heat. Add 2 tbsp butter along with the garlic and cook over moderate heat for 1-2 minutes.

7. Add 1 tbsp of flour to the butter-garlic mixture and gradually pour in the wine while on moderate heat, for 60 seconds.

8. Squeeze the juice of the ¼ lemon into the pan. Add the stock together with the cream.

9. Sprinkle in the Italian seasoning and thyme leaves. Season to taste and simmer for a couple of minutes. Taste, and adjust the seasoning as needed.

10. When you are ready to plate up, reduce the heat to low.

11. Transfer the chops to the pan and reheat, making sure they are sufficiently cooked. Timings will very much depend on the thickness of the meat.

12. Drizzle the sauce over the chops and on low, heat for 2-3 minutes.

Roma-Style Lamb with Rosemary, Sage, and Anchovy

Savor this succulent, Romanesque-style lamb whose flavors are enhanced by a winning combination of herbs and anchovy.

Servings: 4

Total Time: 2hours 20mins

Ingredients:

- 2 tbsp olive oil
- 3⅓ pounds boneless lamb shoulder (cut into 1½" pieces)
- Seasoned plain flour
- 6¾ ounces dry white wine
- ½ cup red wine vinegar
- 4 sprigs of rosemary (roughly chopped)
- 12 sage leaves
- Water
- 3 anchovy fillets
- Sage leaves (to garnish)

Directions:

1. Preheat the main oven to 320 degrees F.

2. Over moderately high heat, heat the olive oil in a large skillet or frying pan.

3. Dust the pieces of lamb in the seasoned flour, shaking off any excess.

4. In batches, fry the meat, occasionally turning, for 3-4 minutes, until golden.

5. Transfer the meat to a sizeable casserole dish.

6. Use the white wine to deglaze the pan, and add to the casserole along with the vinegar, rosemary, and 12 sage leaves. Pour in 13½ ounces of water, to virtually cover the lamb and bring to a simmer before transferring to the oven and cooking while occasionally stirring until tender; this will take between 60-90 minutes.

7. Set to one side to rest for approximately 15-20 minutes.

8. In a pan combine 3½ ounces of braising liquid with the anchovy fillets and over moderate heat, whisk until the anchovies are entirely dissolved. Return the liquid to the lamb mixture, stirring to incorporate.

9. Season and garnish with additional sage leaves.

Sweet Potato and Fennel Curry

Fennel has a mild but intense licorice flavor and fragrance which makes it perfect for a veggie curry dish.

Servings: 4

Total Time: 55mins

Ingredients:

- 4 cups sweet potatoes (peeled, cubed)
- 1 tsp extra-virgin olive oil
- 1 cup fennel (diced)
- 1 cup red onion (peeled, diced)
- 2 tbsp curry powder
- 2 tsp virgin coconut oil
- ¼ tsp sea salt
- 1 cup chickpeas (cooked)
- ¼ cup fresh cilantro (chopped)
- 2 tbsp fresh mint (chopped)
- 2 tbsp sweetened dried cranberries
- 2 tsp extra-virgin olive oil
- Juice from ½ a lemon
- Rice (to serve, optional)

Directions:

1. Preheat the main oven to 400 degrees F.

2. Toss the sweet potatoes in olive lay and arrange on baking sheet.

3. Roast in the oven until the sweet potatoes are fork tender, 30-40 minutes, and set to one side.

4. In the meantime, to a cast iron frying pan or skillet, add the fennel followed by the red onion, curry powder, and coconut oil. Season with salt.

5. Sauté over moderate heat for between 5-7 minutes, or until the fennel and onion is softened. Take care not to overcook.

6. Add the fennel mixture to a mixing bowl along with the chickpeas, cilantro, mint, cranberries, olive oil and lemon juice. Add the roasted potatoes and stir well to coat evenly.

7. Serve with rice.

Vietnamese Lemongrass Chicken

Pounding the chicken ensures super tender and juicy meat and will also speed up cooking time!

Servings: 4

Total Time: 1 hour

Ingredients:

- 1 shallot (chopped)
- 4 stalks lemongrass (outer layers removed, chopped)
- ½ tsp red pepper flakes
- ¼ cup lime juice
- 2 cloves garlic (peeled, chopped)
- 2 tsp brown sugar
- 2 tsp fish sauce
- Salt and black pepper
- 4 boneless, skinless chicken breasts (pounded to ½" thick)
- 2 tbsp canola oil

Directions:

1. Add the shallot, lemongrass, red pepper flakes, lime juice, garlic, brown sugar, and fish sauce to a food processor and blitz until smooth and paste-like.

2. Season the chicken breasts and transfer to a large ziplock bag along with paste. Massage the paste into the chicken and chill for 45 minutes.

3. Place a skillet over moderately high heat. Add the oil, when hot, add the marinated chicken. Cook for several minutes, flip and cook for another couple of minutes, until golden.

4. Serve straight away.

Sauces and Sides

Cucumber and Mint Jelly

This refreshing jelly pairs perfectly with salmon or lamb chops.

Servings: 2-3 cups

Total Time: 55mins

Ingredients:

- 1 pound cucumbers (peeled, cut into chunks)
- 3½ cups sugar
- ½ cup apple cider vinegar
- 3 ounces liquid fruit pectin
- ¼ cup packed fresh mint leaves
- 1 drop green food coloring

Directions:

1. Puree the chunks of cucumber in a food processor.

2. Using the back of a spoon, push the puree through a mesh sieve place over a mixing bowl. Measure out ¾ cup of cucumber juice.

3. In a 3-4 quart heavy pot, combine the juice with the sugar, and apple cider vinegar. Over high heat, bring to boil, while stirring to dissolve the sugar.

4. Quickly add the pectin and mint, stirring to combine.

5. Bring the mixture to boil, continually stirring. Boil fast for 60 seconds.

6. Remove the pot from the heat and skim off any surface foam.

7. With a slotted spoon, discard any mind.

8. Add the food coloring and stir to combine.

9. Carefully, with a ladle, transfer the jelly to sterilized, hot, ¼ pint canning jars, allowing a headspace of ¼".

10. Wipe the rims of the jars, adjust the lids and screw on the bands.

11. Process the filled canning jars in a boiling water canner for 5 minutes (begin to time when the water returns to a boil).

12. Take the jars out of the canner and allow to cool on wire racks.

Garlic Herb Sauce

Use this versatile sauce to either marinate fish, add flavor to soup, or season rice.

Servings: 1½ cups

Total Time: 35mins

Ingredients:

- 1 head garlic (unpeeled, separated into cloves)
- 2 cups (packed) parsley leaves including tender stems
- 1 cup (packed) mint leaves
- 1 cup extra-virgin olive oil
- 1 tbsp + 1 tsp freshly squeezed lemon juice
- 1 tsp lemon zest (finely grated)
- 1 tsp crushed red pepper flakes
- ¾ tsp kosher salt

Directions:

1. Heat a dry and heavy frying pan or skillet over moderate heat.

2. Add the garlic and roast while occasionally stirring until the garlic skins have darkened and the cloves are softened. This will take between 12-15 minutes. Set aside to cool.

3. Peel and discard the skins.

4. Transfer the garlic cloves to a food blender and add the parsley followed by the mint, olive oil, freshly squeezed lemon juice and zest along with the red pepper flakes and kosher salt and process to a pesto-like sauce.

Cook's Note: This sauce can be made up to 5 days ahead. Store in a resealable, airtight container and either freeze or chill for up to 30 days.

Grilled Corn with a Mixed Herb Dressing

A handful of fresh ingredients and a light dressing make this grilled corn a healthy side dish.

Servings: 4

Total Time: 1hour 20mins

Ingredients:

- 4 ears of sweet corn in husks
- 1 tbsp salt (for soaking)

Herb Dressing:

- 1 cup extra-virgin olive oil
- 2 tbsp sweet onion (diced)
- ½ cup fresh cilantro (chopped)
- ½ cup fresh parsley (chopped)
- 2 tbsp fresh chives (chopped)
- 2 tsp freshly squeezed lemon juice
- Salt and fresh cracked pepper

Directions:

1. Peel back the husks from the corn ears, taking care not to tear them. Pull away the corn silk and lift the husks back over the corn.

2. In a mixing bowl, soak the corn in sufficient water to cover, along with 1 tbsp of salt. Set to one side to soak for 60 seconds.

3. In a shallow bowl, combine the oil with the onion, cilantro, parsley, chives, and lemon juice. Season with a pinch of salt and a dash of pepper and set to one side at room temperature while you grill the corn. When the corn is sufficiently soaked, preheat the grill to a moderate or moderate to low setting. Do this with the lid firmly closed.

4. Drain any excess water from the corn and arrange onto the grilling grate.

5. Close the lid of the grill and cook for between 15-10 minutes, remember to rotate every 4-5 minutes. The corn is ready when the kernels are bite tender.

6. Remove and discard any remaining husk.

7. Serve the grilled corn with a side of herb dressing.

Hasselback Sweet Potatoes with Compound Mixed Herb Ghee

Compound ghee is a fancy name for ghee flavored with herbs, seasonings or any other aromatic ingredient. As a sweet potato topping, it transforms this side dish from good to great!

Servings: 2-4

Total Time: 1hour 12mins

Ingredients:

- Sweet Potatoes:
- 1 pound white sweet potatoes (scrubbed)
- 1 tbsp ghee (melted)
- 1 tsp sea salt
- Compound Mixed Herb Ghee:
- 2 tbsp ghee (room temperature)
- 1 garlic clove (peeled, finely chopped)
- 1 sprig of fresh rosemary (chopped)
- 5 sprigs of fresh thyme

Directions:

1. Preheat the main oven to 400 degrees F. Using parchment paper, line a baking sheet.

2. Take a sharp knife and make 6-7 vertical cuts in the potatoes. Start from the top and cut most of the way down. Stop cutting approximately ¼" from the bottom.

3. Arrange the potatoes on the prepared baking sheet.

4. Brush the potatoes with the melted ghee and season with salt.

5. Transfer to the oven for 1-1¼ hours, or until the potatoes are fork tender.

6. In the meantime, and while the potatoes bakes, in a bowl combine the ghee together with the garlic, rosemary, and thyme. Using a hand mixer, whip until a soft and fluffy mixture forms.

7. Top the baked potatoes with the compound mixed herb ghee and enjoy.

Lemon Balm Pesto

Lemon balm pesto is particularly good with seafood, fish or potatoes. Lemon balm, which is a member of the mint family, has long been used in herbal medicine to improve sleep and relieve anxiety.

Servings: 1 cup

Total Time: 10mins

Ingredients:

- ¾ cup packed lemon balm leaves
- ½ cup pine nuts
- ¾ cup Parmesan
- ¼ cup extra virgin olive oil
- 3 tbsp freshly squeezed lemon juice
- 1 tsp fresh chives
- Salt and pepper

Directions:

1. Add the lemon balm leaves, pine nuts, Parmesan, oil, freshly squeezed lemon juice, and chives to a blender and process until silky smooth. Taste and season.

2. Store the pesto in an airtight container in the fridge for up to 7 days.

Pan-Fried Carrots with Lemon and Marjoram

This flavorful side dish is good to serve alongside fish, poultry or meat. Marjoram's sweet pine and citrus flavors give added zing to this simple dish.

Servings: 4

Total Time: 20mins

Ingredients:

- 3 tbsp olive oil (divided)
- 1 large, garlic clove (peeled, minced)
- 2 pounds carrots (diagonally cut into ½" slices)
- 1 tsp sugar
- ½ tsp salt (divided)
- ¼ tsp freshly ground black pepper
- 1 tbsp fresh marjoram (chopped)
- 4 tsp freshly squeezed lemon juice

Directions:

1. In a pan, heat 1½ tbsp of oil over moderate-low heat.

2. Add the garlic along with the carrots, sugar, ¼ tsp of salt, pepper, and marjoram. Cover and cook while occasionally stirring for 5 minutes.

3. Remove the lid from the pan and increase the heat to medium and cook while frequently stirring, until the carrots are fork tender and browned, this will take an additional 6-8 minutes.

4. Take the pan off the heat.

5. Stir in the remaining oil along with ¼ tsp of salt followed by the freshly squeezed lemon juice and serve.

Roasted Beets with Pistachios, Mixed Herbs, and Orange

Wow your guests with this colorful side which makes a welcome change from regular green salads.

Servings: 8

Total Time: 1hour 20mins

Ingredients:

- 3 pounds medium beets
- 1 (3") cinnamon stick (snapped into 4 pieces)
- 2 bay leaves
- 1 cup water
- 1 large shallot (minced)
- ¼ cup white wine vinegar
- Salt
- Zest of 1 orange (finely grated)
- ¼ cup chopped tarragon
- ¼ cup chopped chives
- ¼ cup chopped flat-leaf parsley
- ¼ cup + 2 tbsp extra-virgin olive oil
- ¼ cup roasted, unsalted pistachios (chopped)
- ¼ cup celery leaves (to garnish)

Directions:

1. Preheat the main oven to 375 degrees F.

2. Arrange the beets in a roasting tin and add the pieces of cinnamon followed by the bay leaves and water.

3. Using aluminum foil, tightly cover the tin and bake in the oven for 60 minutes, or until the beets are fork tender. Transfer the beets to a baking sheet and set aside to cool, discarding the herbs, spices, and liquid.

4. In the meantime, in a mixing bowl, combine the shallot with the vinegar. Add a pinch of salt and set aside to rest for 10 minutes.

5. Add the orange zest, tarragon, chives, parsley and oil and stir to incorporate. Season with a pinch of salt.

6. Peel, trim and slice the beets. They should be no more than approximately ¼" thick.

7. Place the slices of beet on a serving platter in rows, overlapping one another.

8. Give the herb dressing a quick stir and spoon or pour it over the beets.

9. Garnish with pistachios.

10. Arrange the celery leaves on the top and enjoy.

Roasted Cauliflower with Herbs and Spices

Pep up cauliflower with herbs and spices and roast in the oven for a great midweek side.

Servings: 2-4

Total Time: 55mins

Ingredients:

- 1 head cauliflower (chopped into bite-size florets)
- 4 cloves garlic (peeled, minced)
- Zest of 1 medium lemon
- 2 tsp cumin
- 2 tsp coriander
- 1 tsp paprika
- ½ tsp red pepper flakes
- ½ tsp kosher salt
- 1 tbsp olive oil
- Freshly ground black pepper
- Lemon wedge (to squeeze)

Directions:

1. Preheat the main oven to 450 degrees F.

2. In a bowl, combine the florets with the garlic and lemon zest followed by the cumin, coriander, paprika, red pepper flakes, kosher salt, olive oil and a few grinds of black pepper. Stir well to coat evenly.

3. Using parchment paper, line a baking sheet.

4. Arrange the cauliflower on the sheet and bake until fork tender, this will take around 40 minutes. Occasionally stir during the cooking process.

5. When you are ready to serve, squeeze with fresh lemon juice. Season to taste and serve warm.

Summer Savory Green Beans with Mushrooms and Bacon

Not dissimilar to thyme or marjoram, summer savory has a pepper-like flavor with a spicy aroma and is ideal for adding pizzazz to green beans.

Servings: 4

Total Time: 20mins

Ingredients:

- 1 pound fresh green beans (trimmed)
- 1½ cups fresh mushrooms (sliced)
- 2 tbsp green onion (chopped)
- 2 tbsp butter
- 2 tbsp fresh summery savory (minced)
- 2 tbsp fresh parsley (minced)
- 1 tbsp freshly squeezed lemon juice
- 1 tbsp cider vinegar
- 1 tbsp canola oil
- 1 tsp sugar
- 1 tsp salt
- ⅛ tsp pepper
- 4 bacon strips (cooked, crumbled)

Directions:

1. Add the beans to a steamer basket and place in a pan over 1" depth of water. Bring to boil, and cover with a lid and steam until crisp-tender, for 7-9 minutes.

2. In the meantime, in a large frying pan or skillet, sauté the mushrooms and onion in the butter until fork tender.

3. Remove the pan from the heat and stir in the summer savory followed by the parsley, freshly squeezed lemon juice, vinegar, oil, sugar, salt, and pepper.

4. Add the beans, tossing to coat.

5. Garnish with bacon crumbles.

Take-Out Kebab Garlic Sauce

Whether you serve it with French fries or slather it over a kebab, one thing's for sure, you and your family will love this garlic infused sauce.

Servings: 4

Total Time: 12mins

Ingredients:

- 1 garlic clove
- Salt
- 2 tbsp mayonnaise
- 2 tbsp yogurt
- Zest of ½ lemon
- Black pepper

Directions:

1. First, fill a kettle with water and bring to boil. Alternatively, bring a pan of water to boil over the stove.

2. Thinly slice the garlic and add it to a sieve.

3. Carefully, pour the boiling water over the sliced garlic.

4. Using the back of a blunt knife, crush the garlic. Add a pinch of salt and crush until a paste forms.

5. In a bowl, combine the garlic paste with the mayonnaise, yogurt, and lemon zest.

6. Taste and season.

7. Serve chilled.

Desserts

Bay Leaf Rice Pudding with Golden Raisins

Thick and creamy rice pudding gently infused with bay leaf and packed full of juicy golden raisins is comfort food at its finest.

Servings: 4-6

Total Time: 1hour 30mins

Ingredients:

- Butter (for dish)
- 3½ cups whole milk
- ⅓ cup Arborio rice
- Pinch kosher salt
- 1 bay leaf
- ⅓ cup white sugar
- ½ cup heavy cream
- 1 tsp vanilla essence
- ¼ cup currants
- ¼ cup golden raisins

Directions:

1. Preheat the main oven to 350 degrees F. Grease a 1½-quart baking dish with butter. Set to one side.

2. Add the milk, rice, salt, bay leaf, and sugar to a saucepan over moderate heat. Bring to a near boil, then turn down to a strong simmer for just over 10 minutes, occasionally stirring, until the rice is al dente. Remove the bay leaf.

3. Pour the heavy cream into a saucepan over high heat and cook until scolded. Take off the heat and stir in the vanilla essence. Allow to cool.

4. Stir the cooled cream into the rice mixture and fold in the currants and raisins. Spoon the mixture into the baking dish.

5. Place in the oven and cook for just over 20 minutes.

6. Serve warm*.

*For a thicker consistency, allow the pudding to stand for 1-2 days.

Bitter Chocolate Basil Tart

A rich and indulgent dessert guaranteed to impress any chocolate connoisseur. Serve with a dollop of fluffy whip cream to lighten up the dish.

Servings: 16

Total Time: 1hour

Ingredients:

- ⅓ cup whole milk
- 1 cup heavy cream
- ½ cup basil leaves (shredded finely)
- 8 ounces bittersweet chocolate (chopped)
- 1 medium egg
- 1 (9") prepared tart shell
- Whip cream (for serving)

Directions:

1. Preheat the main oven to 375 degrees F.

2. Add the milk, cream, and basil to a saucepan over moderate heat and bring to a near boil. Take off the heat and set to one side for 10 minutes.

3. Add the chopped chocolate to a bowl and strain over the milk mixture. Stir well until the chocolate melts. Allow to cool.

4. Whisk the egg into the chocolate mixture until smooth and combined. Pour into the tart shell.

5. Place in the oven and bake for 20 minutes until almost set.

6. Allow to cool completely before slicing and serving with whip cream.

Citrus Sorrel Sherbet

For a fun summertime treat, try serving a scoop of citrus sorrel sherbet in a martini glass topped with Prosecco!

Servings: 8

Total Time: 6hours 15mins

Ingredients:

- Juice of 5 medium lemons
- 1¼ tsp flavorless gelatine powder
- 1½ cups water
- 1½ cups white sugar
- 5-6 sorrel leaves
- 2¼ cups whole milk
- 2 tsp lemon zest

Directions:

1. Add the lemon juice to a bowl and sprinkle with the gelatine. Set aside for 5-6 minutes.

2. Add the water and sugar to a saucepan over moderate heat and bring to a boil, turn down to a simmer and cook for 3-4 minutes until the sugar dissolves.

3. Take off the heat and stir in the gelatine/lemon mixture. Chill for a couple of hours.

4. Add the sorrel, milk, and lemon zest to a blender along with the chilled lemon syrup. Blitz until smooth.

5. Transfer to an ice cream maker and churn according to manufacturer instructions.

6. After churning, transfer to a re-sealable container and freeze for a few hours before serving.

Lavender and Walnut Blondies

Moist and chewy blondies with the floral aroma of lavender and pieces of crunchy walnut are a little slice of heaven.

Servings: 8

Total Time: 1hour

Ingredients:

- ⅛ tsp bicarb of soda
- ½ tsp baking powder
- 1 cup all-purpose flour
- ½ tsp kosher salt
- 1 cup brown sugar
- ⅓ cup unsalted butter (melted)
- 1 tbsp vanilla essence
- 1 medium egg
- 1½ tbsp culinary-grade lavender (minced)
- ½ cup walnuts (chopped)

Directions:

1. Preheat the main oven to 350 degrees F.

2. Combine the bicarb of soda, baking powder, flour, and salt in a bowl.

3. In a second bowl, whisk together the sugar, butter, vanilla, and egg.

4. Fold the flour mixture into the butter mixture until combined.

5. Stir in the lavender and walnut.

6. Pour the blondie batter into an 8" baking tin and place in the oven. Bake for just over 20 minutes until golden.

7. Allow to completely cool before slicing and serving.

Nectarine Thyme Crumble

A mouth-watering dessert packed to bursting with fresh juicy nectarines is the ultimate summer pick-me-up.

Servings: 6

Total Time: 1hour 30mins

Ingredients:

- 6 ripe nectarines (stoned, sliced)
- 1½ tbsp fresh lemon juice
- 6 tbsp white sugar
- Salt
- 6 thyme sprigs
- 4 tbsp brown sugar
- ¾ cup all-purpose flour
- 2 tbsp wheat germ
- ¼ cup unsalted butter (chopped)

Directions:

1. Toss the nectarine in the lemon juice, sugar, salt, and thyme. Set aside for 60 minutes.

2. Preheat the main oven to 375 degrees F.

3. Combine the brown sugar, flour, and wheat germ in a second bowl. Rub the butter into the mixture until crumbly. Transfer to a baking sheet.

4. Divide the nectarine mixture between 6 small cast-iron dishes. Place in the oven and bake for 20 minutes.

5. For the last 10 minutes of cooking, place the baking sheet of crumble in the oven.

6. Sprinkle the baked crumbled equally over the cooked fruit and bake for a final 5 minutes. Serve.

Pineapple Mint Granita

Transport yourself to an Island beach with this tropical pineapple and mint granita.

Servings: 8

Total Time: 7hours 10mins

Ingredients:

- 3 mint sprigs
- 1 cup boiling water
- 1 cup ice water
- 4 cups fresh pineapple juice
- 2-3 tbsp agave nectar

Directions:

1. Add the mint to a bowl and pour over the boiling water.

2. Remove the mint from the bowl and plunge it into the ice water. After 10 seconds, remove the mint from the ice water and pat dry with kitchen paper before chopping.

3. Add the chopped mint to the pineapple juice and stir in the agave nectar.

4. Transfer to a 13x9" dish and freeze for 3 hours. Remove from the freezer, fluff up using a fork and freeze for another 3-4 hours before serving.

Rosemary Melon Sorbet

This refreshing sorbet is the ideal treat for those hot summer days. What's more, it can be whipped up in just 5 minutes!

Servings: 4-6

Total Time: 8hours 5mins

Ingredients:

- 3-4 cups winter melon (chopped)
- ¾ tsp fresh rosemary (minced)
- 2 tbsp agave syrup

Directions:

1. Arrange the melon on a baking sheet and pop in the freezer overnight.

2. The following day, add the melon to a food processor along with the rosemary and agave syrup. Blitz until combined.

3. Spoon into bowls and serve straight away.

Sage and Cranberry Cookies

Melt-in-the-mouth buttery cookies are the ideal after-dinner treat to serve with tea or coffee.

Servings: 22

Total Time: 1hour 30mins

Ingredients:

- 1 cup salted butter (at room temperature)
- 2 tbsp cornstarch
- ½ cup confectioner's sugar
- 1½ cups all-purpose flour
- 1 tsp vanilla
- 1 tbsp fresh sage (chopped)
- ½ cup dried, sweetened cranberries (roughly chopped)

Directions:

1. Whisk the butter, using an electric mixer, for a couple of minutes until fluffy.

2. Whisk in the cornstarch and confectioner's sugar until well combined.

3. Add the flour and continue to mix until incorporated.

4. Stir in the vanilla essence.

5. Finally, fold in the sage and cranberries.

6. Using clean hands, form the cookie dough into a ball, cover with plastic wrap and chill for 60 minutes.

7. Preheat the main oven to 375 degrees F.

8. Lightly flour your worktop. Roll the chilled dough into a ⅛" thick sheet. Use a 2" cookie cutter to cut circles from the dough and arrange on cookie sheets.

9. Place in the oven and bake for 7-8 minutes, until pale golden and set.

10. Allow to completely cool before serving.

Tarragon Berry Tumble with Anise Oat Topping

The unique licorice flavor of tarragon and anise complement fresh summer berries perfectly.

Servings: 6

Total Time: 1hour 20mins

Ingredients:

Topping:

- ¼ cup buckwheat flour
- 2 cups rolled oats
- 2 tbsp pure maple syrup
- ¼ cup melted coconut oil
- ½ tsp crushed anise seeds
- 2 tsp chia seeds
- ¼ tsp kosher salt

Berry Tumble:

- ¼ cup fresh orange juice
- 4 cups mixed summer berries
- 2 tsp cornstarch
- 2 tbsp fresh tarragon (chopped)

Directions:

1. Preheat the main oven to 350 degrees F.

2. First, make the topping. Combine the flour, oats, maple syrup, coconut oil, anise, chia seeds, and salt in a bowl. Set to one side.

3. Next, make the berry mixture. Stir together the juice, berries, cornstarch, and tarragon.

4. Spoon the berry mixture into an 8" square dish.

5. Spoon the oat mixture on top of the berries.

6. Place in the oven and bake for approximately 40 minutes until golden. Serve warm.

Vanilla and Garlic Ice Cream

Yes, really! Just a small amount of garlic can transform homemade vanilla ice cream into an unforgettable delicacy.

Servings: 8

Total Time: 8hours 15mins

- 1 garlic cloves (peeled, minced)
- 2 cups whole milk
- 1 vanilla pod (seeds scraped and pod reserved)
- 1½ cups white sugar
- 1 cup heavy cream
- Yolks of 8 large eggs

Directions:

1. Add the garlic, milk, vanilla seeds, and pods in a saucepan over moderate heat and bring to boil. Take off the heat straight away.

2. In a clean bowl, whisk together the sugar, cream, and yolks.

3. While whisking the egg mixture, slowly strain in the hot milk. Transfer the mixture to the saucepan and gently cook for just over 10 minutes until the mixture easily coasts the back of a spoon.

4. Transfer to a re-sealable container and refrigerate until well chilled.

5. Pour into an ice cream maker and churn according to manufacturer's instructions.

6. Scoop the ice cream back into the re-sealable container and freeze for 3-4 hours until firm.

Author's Afterthoughts

Thanks ever so much to each of my cherished readers for investing the time to read this book!

I know you could have picked from many other books but you chose this one. So a big thanks for downloading this book and reading all the way to the end.

If you enjoyed this book or received value from it, I'd like to ask you for a favor. Please take a few minutes to post an honest and heartfelt review on Amazon.com. Your support does make a difference and helps to benefit other people.

Thanks!

Daniel Humphreys

About the Author

Daniel Humphreys

Many people will ask me if I am German or Norman, and my answer is that I am 100% unique! Joking aside, I owe my cooking influence mainly to my mother who was British!   I can certainly make a mean Sheppard's pie, but when it comes to preparing Bratwurst sausages and drinking beer with friends, I am also all in!

I am taking you on this culinary journey with me and hope you can appreciate my diversified background. In my 15 years career as a chef, I never had a dish returned to me by one of clients, so that should say something about me! Actually, I will take that back. My worst critic is my four years old son, who refuses to taste anything that is green color. That shall pass, I am sure.

My hope is to help my children discover the joy of cooking and sharing their creations with their loved ones, like I did all my life. When you develop a passion for cooking and my suspicious is that you have one as well, it usually sticks for life. The best advice I can give anyone as a professional chef is invest. Invest your time, your heart in each meal you are creating. Invest also a little money in good cooking hardware and quality ingredients. But most of all enjoy every meal you prepare with YOUR friends and family!

Printed in Great Britain
by Amazon

85508150R00079